560
Rose Doré
(Alizarin)

CW01033380

OIL PAINTER'S POCKET PALETTE

Practical visual guidance to over 600 colour mixes

Rosalind Cuthbert

SEARCH PRESS

A QUARTO BOOK

Published in paperback
2000 by
Search Press Ltd
Wellwood
North Farm Road
Tunbridge Wells
Kent TN2 3DR
United Kingdom

Reprinted 2001, 2003

ISBN 0 85532 941 6

Conceived, designed
and produced by
Quarto Publishing plc
6 Blundell Street
London
N7 9BH

Printed in China by
Leefung-Asco Printers

THE COLOURS

Monestial blue
page **13**

Prussian blue
page **14**

Monestial
turquoise
page **15**

Oxide of
chromium green
page **23**

Lemon yellow
page **28**

Cadmium yellow
page **29**

Raw sienna
page **33**

Cadmium red
page **38**

Alizarin crimson
page **39**

Rose doré
page **43**

Permanent
magenta
page **48**

Permanent mauve
page **49**

Vandyke brown
page **53**

Payne's grey
page **58**

Ivory black
page **59**

CONTENTS

How To Use This Book

For the beginner to oil painting, it may take a considerable degree of trial and error to discover which colours you can mix in order to obtain particular effects, and this can be both frustrating and wasteful of paint. The purpose of this book is to cut down on learning time by providing the oil painter with a visual guide to over 300 different colour mixtures and over 700 tint variations, achieved by the addition of white in varying proportions. Beginners will thus find the book invaluable, while more experienced painters may discover some new combinations.

Oil paint is usually thought of as an opaque medium, but it can be made transparent by the addition of various mediums, and colours can be "mixed" on the painting surface

THE SYMBOLS

Permanent

Normally permanent

Moderately permanent

Transparent

Semi-transparent

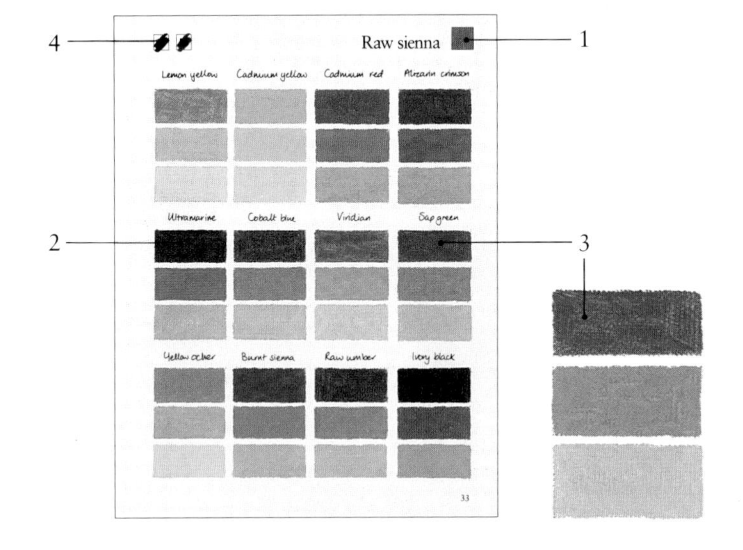
4
Raw sienna
1
Lemon yellow
Cadmium yellow
Cadmium red
Alizarin crimson
Ultramarine
Cobalt blue
Viridian
Sap green
2
3
Yellow ocher
Burnt sienna
Raw umber
Ivory black
33

▲ *Each page of colour charts features one of the 30 colours chosen for this book, referred to as the main colour (1). For a visual guide to these, see pages 2 and 3. Each of the main colours is mixed with a constant basic palette (2) of 12 colours, which are repeated in the same order on every page. Each colour combination is shown first as a pure mixture and then mixed with white in two different proportions (3), first approximately 50/50 and then 80/20. The symbol (4) denotes the degree of permanence of the main colour and shows whether it is transparent or semi-transparent (see pages 8-9).*

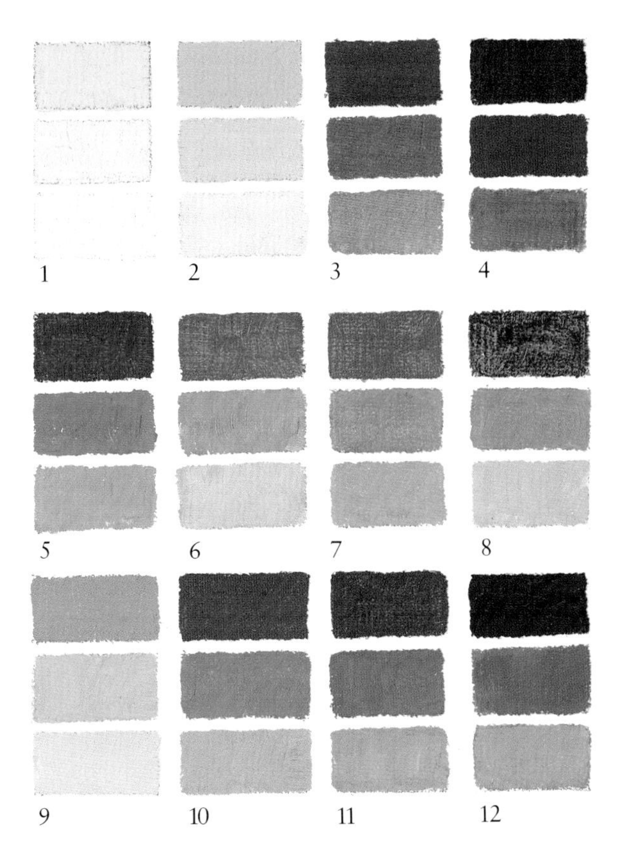
1
2
3
4
5
6
7
8
9
10
11
12

◀ *This is the basic palette used throughout the book, shown here without the addition of the main colour. The top band shows the pure colour, while white has been added for the other two.*

1 *Lemon yellow*
2 *Cadmium yellow*
3 *Cadmium red*
4 *Alizarin crimson*
5 *Ultramarine*
6 *Cobalt blue*
7 *Viridian*
8 *Sap green*
9 *Yellow ochre*
10 *Burnt sienna*
11 *Raw umber*
12 *Ivory black*

REMEMBER

Each main colour is featured on its own page. The basic palette repeats once on every page.

by overlaying one over another. This technique, called glazing, is shown in a special feature, on pages 60-61, but in the charts which form the core of the book, the paint is shown in its opaque form, without the addition of any medium. The colours shown in the charts are from the Daler-Rowney range of Artist's Oil Colours, used on Daler canvas board.

THE BASIC PALETTE

Professional artists seldom use a large range of colours, preferring to gain their effects through mixing. Some use no more than five colours, and a perfectly satisfactory picture can be painted with only the three primaries (see page 6) plus white and possibly black. Our basic palette contains 12 colours, giving many possible permutations. This is only a suggested list; if you wish you may substitute colours.

PRIMARY, SECONDARY AND TERTIARY COLOURS

Excluding white and black, there are only three colours that cannot be made from mixtures of other colours. These are red, yellow and blue, which are known as the three primary colours. Mixtures of two primaries, blue and yellow, which makes green, are called secondary colours. But as you can see from the colour wheel, there are different versions of each primary, and your secondary colour will depend on which red, blue or yellow is used.

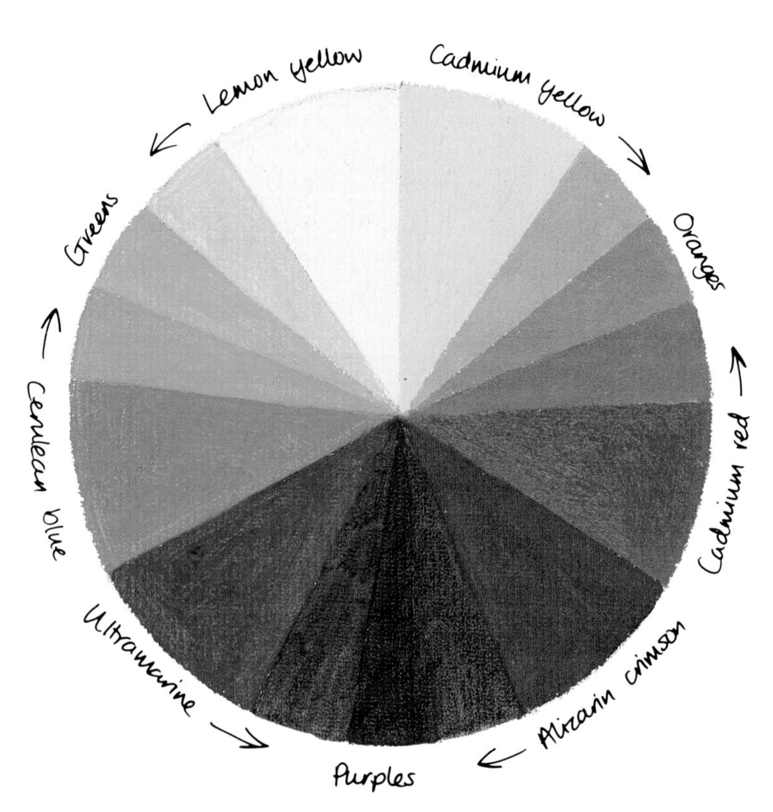
Lemon yellow
Cadmium yellow
Oranges
Cadmium red
Alizarin crimson
Purples
Ultramarine
Cerulean blue
Greens

THE COLOUR WHEEL

▲ *This simple wheel shows two versions of each primary colour, and the secondaries mixed from the two primaries to right and left of them. As you can see, the most vivid secondaries are made from the primaries which have a slight bias towards each other. A bright orange, for example, is made from cadmium red, which leans towards yellow, and cadmium yellow, which has a slight red bias.*

COLOUR INTENSITY

▶ *Although purples, oranges and greens (secondaries) can be mixed from primaries, it is not always possible to mix as vivid a secondary colour as you can purchase in a tube. Cadmium orange, for instance, is brighter than a mixture of cadmium red and cadmium yellow, and permanent mauve is brighter than most mixtures of blue and red.*

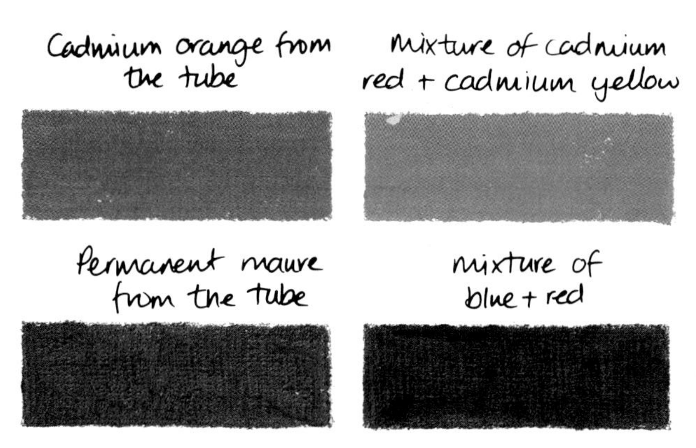

Cadmium orange from the tube
Mixture of cadmium red + cadmium yellow
Permanent mauve from the tube
mixture of blue + red

The tertiary colours are the neutrals, such as browns and most greys except those made with black and white. They are called tertiary because they contain all the three primary colours. This does not mean they are necessarily mixtures of three colours; they can be made from one secondary (i.e. two primaries) and one primary colour.

COMPLEMENTARY COLOURS

These are the colours opposite one another on the colour wheel: red and green; yellow and mauve; blue and orange. They are important in painting because they set up vibrant effects, but curiously, when these pairs are mixed together they cancel each other out, producing neutral colours. Some of these mixtures are shown on pages 34-35.

Yellow
Purple
Orange
Blue
Red
Green

OPACITY AND STRENGTH OF COLOUR

Another important thing to understand when you are mixing colours is that different pigments have different properties, some being more opaque than others. This affects their mixing capabilities, and if used unmixed, their ability to cover an underlying colour. Opaque pigments such as oxide of chromium green have strong covering power, while sap green is transparent, and instead of obliterating a colour below, it will modify it by adding its own quality. You can see some of these differences in the chart below.

Lemon yellow
Cadmium yellow
Rose doré
Cadmium red
Cobalt blue.
Ultramarine
Painted very thinly
Slightly thicker layer
Thick layer

	Colour as in the tube	10% white added	50% white added	90% white added
Lemon yellow				
Cadmium yellow				
Rose doré				
Alizarin crimson				
Cerulean blue				
Ultramarine				
Sap green				
Oxide of chromium				

In the context of colour mixing, an even more important factor is the strength of the colour. Some colours will dominate others in a mixture, and have to be used in smaller amounts. Strength of colour is not related to opacity. Alizarin crimson, for example, is very strong but transparent, while cerulean blue is weak but semi-opaque. A transparent colour can be made opaque by adding white, but its strength will determine how much it is lightened in the process.

When white is added to a colour it often has the effect of cooling it as well as lightening it. As you can see from the chart above, this is particularly noticeable with the reds, which change from warm, vivid colours to quite cool pinks. This is because the warm end of the spectrum of light is partially blocked by the white pigment, leaving a higher proportion of cooler light rays (i.e. more blue).

Cobalt blue

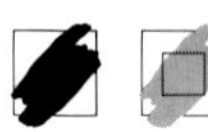

Lemon yellow
Cadmium yellow
Cadmium red
Alizarin crimson
Ultramarine
Cobalt blue
Viridian
Sap green
Yellow ochre
Burnt sienna
Raw umber
Ivory black

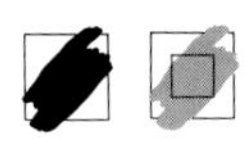

Cerulean blue

Lemon yellow

Cadmium yellow

Cadmium red

Alizarin crimson

Ultramarine

Cobalt blue

Viridian

Sap green

Yellow ochre

Burnt sienna

Raw umber

Ivory black

Ultramarine

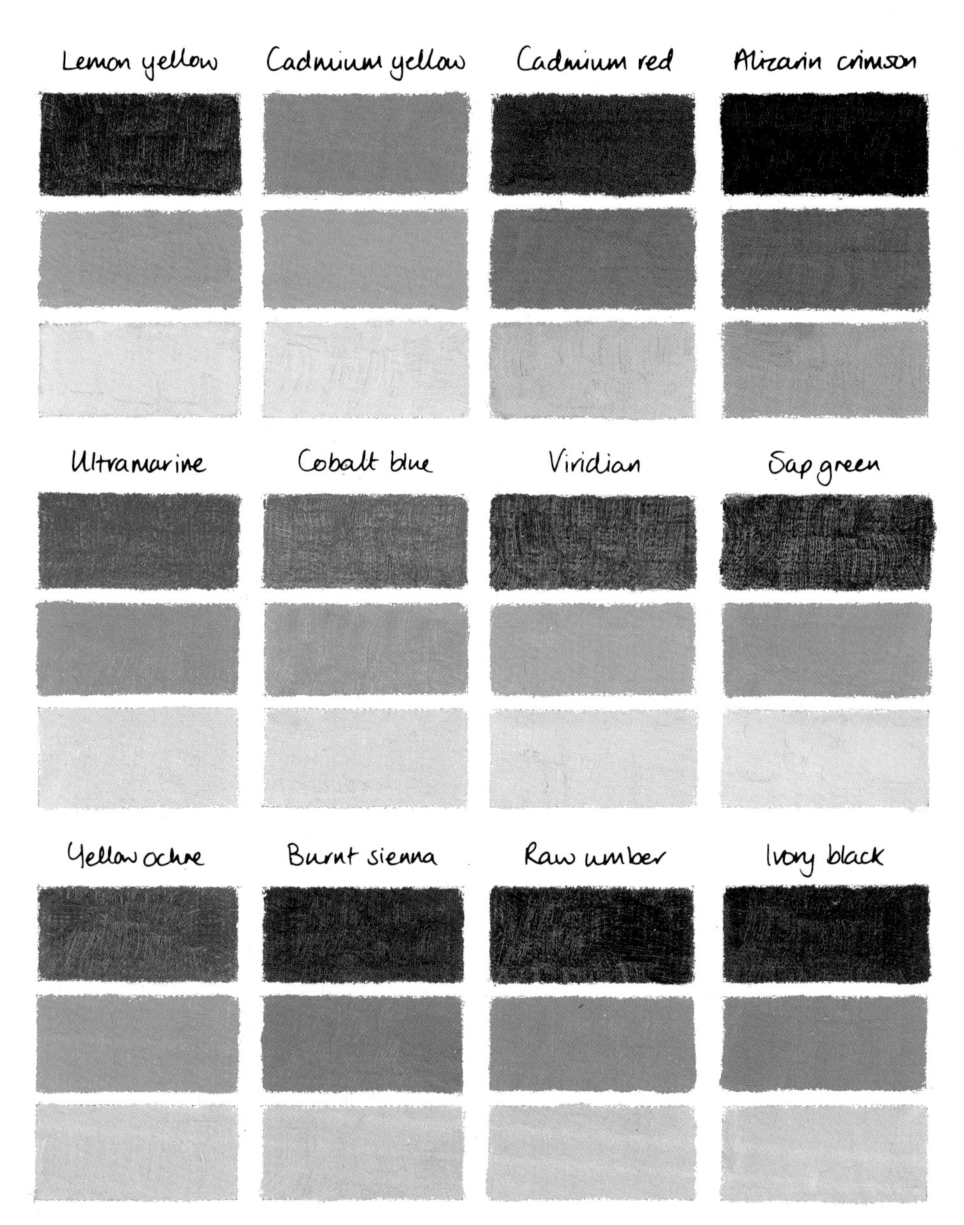
Lemon yellow
Cadmium yellow
Cadmium red
Alizarin crimson
Ultramarine
Cobalt blue
Viridian
Sap green
Yellow ochre
Burnt sienna
Raw umber
Ivory black

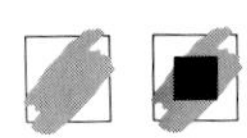

Monestial blue

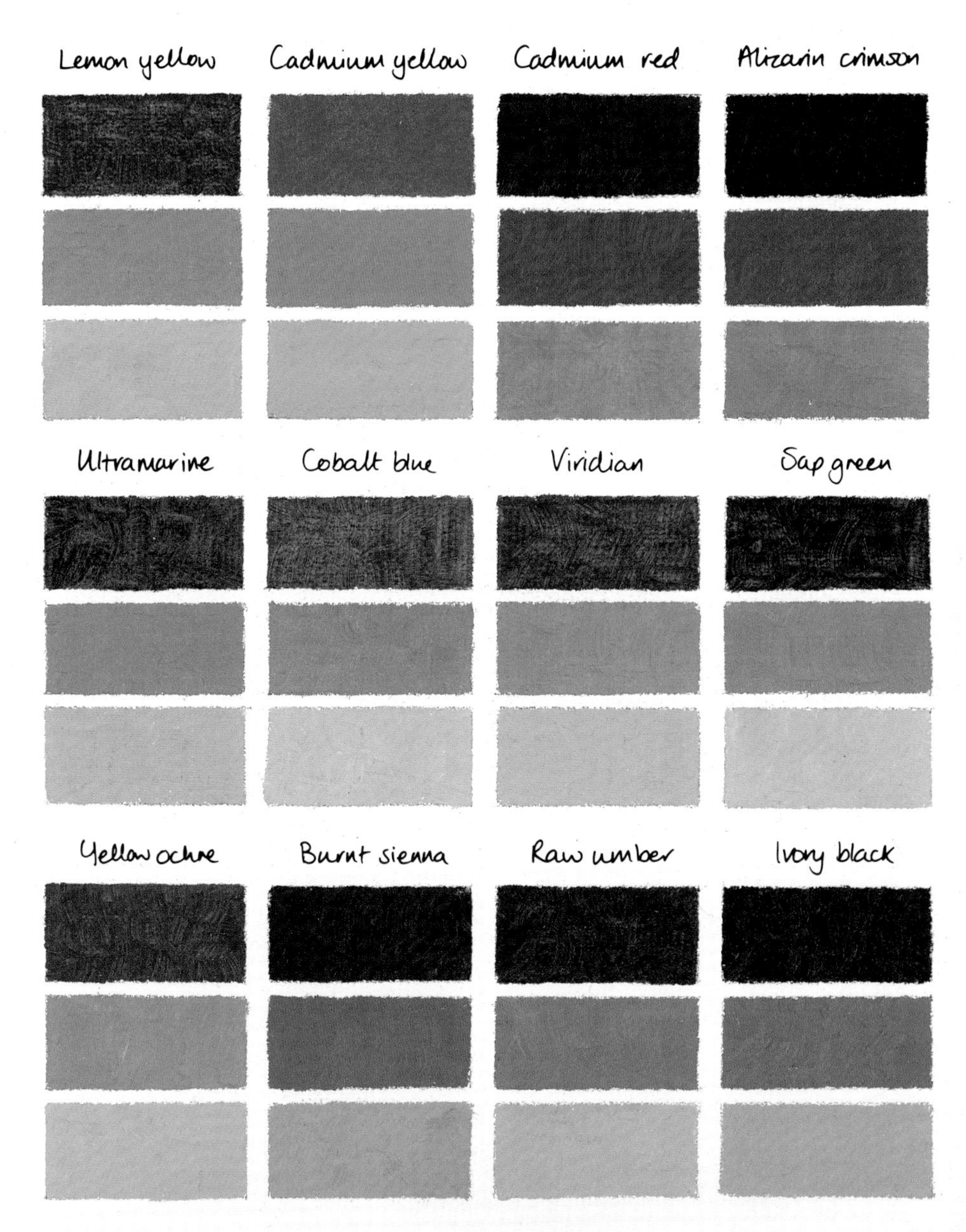
Lemon yellow
Cadmium yellow
Cadmium red
Alizarin crimson
Ultramarine
Cobalt blue
Viridian
Sap green
Yellow ochre
Burnt sienna
Raw umber
Ivory black

Prussian blue

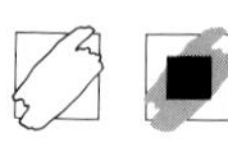

Lemon yellow
Cadmium yellow
Cadmium red
Alizarin crimson
Ultramarine
Cobalt blue
Viridian
Sap green
Yellow ochre
Burnt sienna
Raw umber
Ivory black

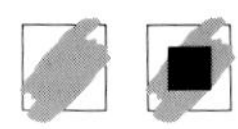

Monestial turquoise

Lemon yellow
Cadmium yellow
Cadmium red
Alizarin crimson
Ultramarine
Cobalt blue
Viridian
Sap green
Yellow ochre
Burnt sienna
Raw umber
Ivory black

Mixing oranges

In these special feature charts, the proportions of the mixes

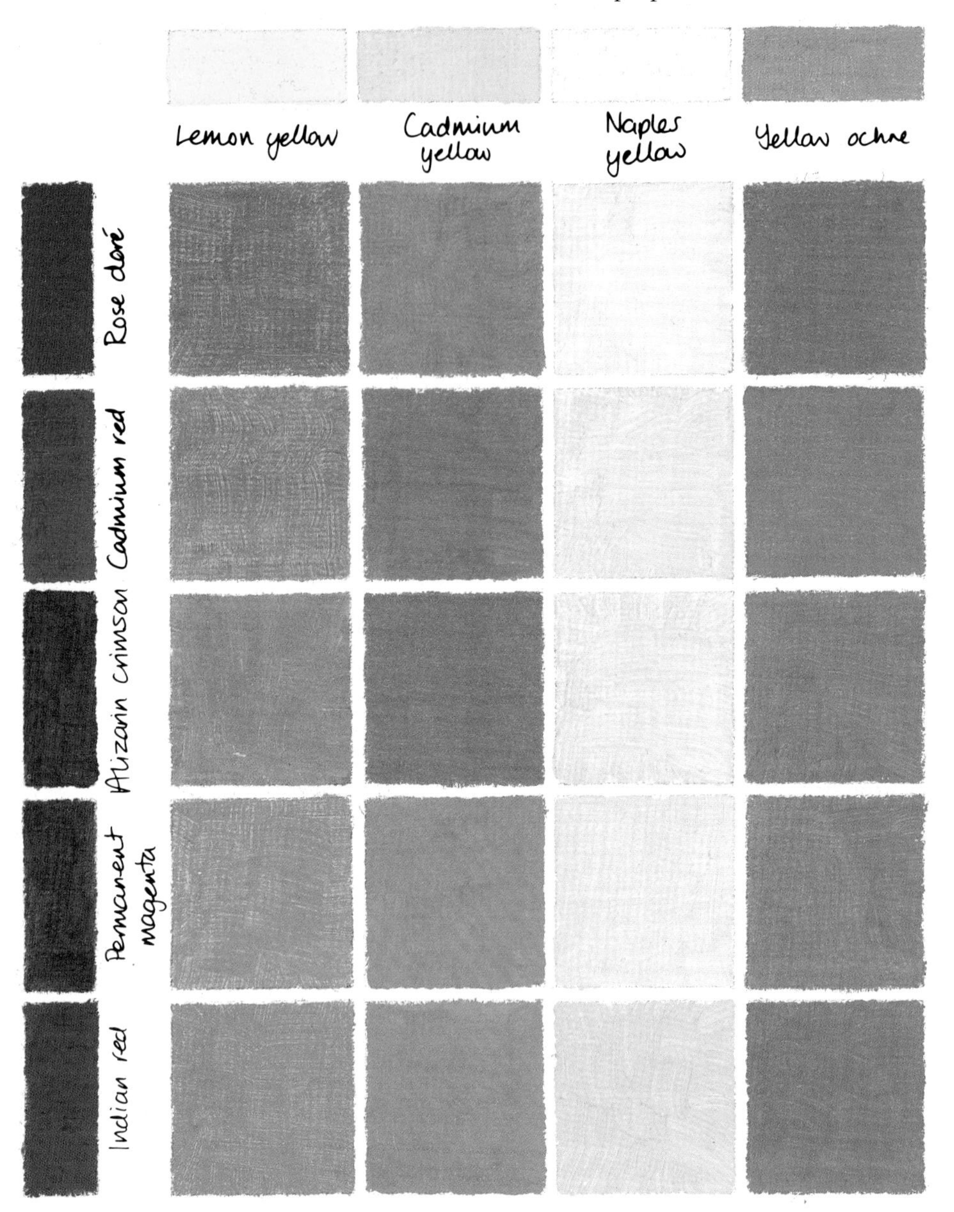

Lemon yellow
Cadmium yellow
Naples yellow
Yellow ochre
Rose doré
Cadmium red
Alizarin crimson
Permanent magenta
Indian red

vary and have been chosen to obtain the best result.

Mixing purples

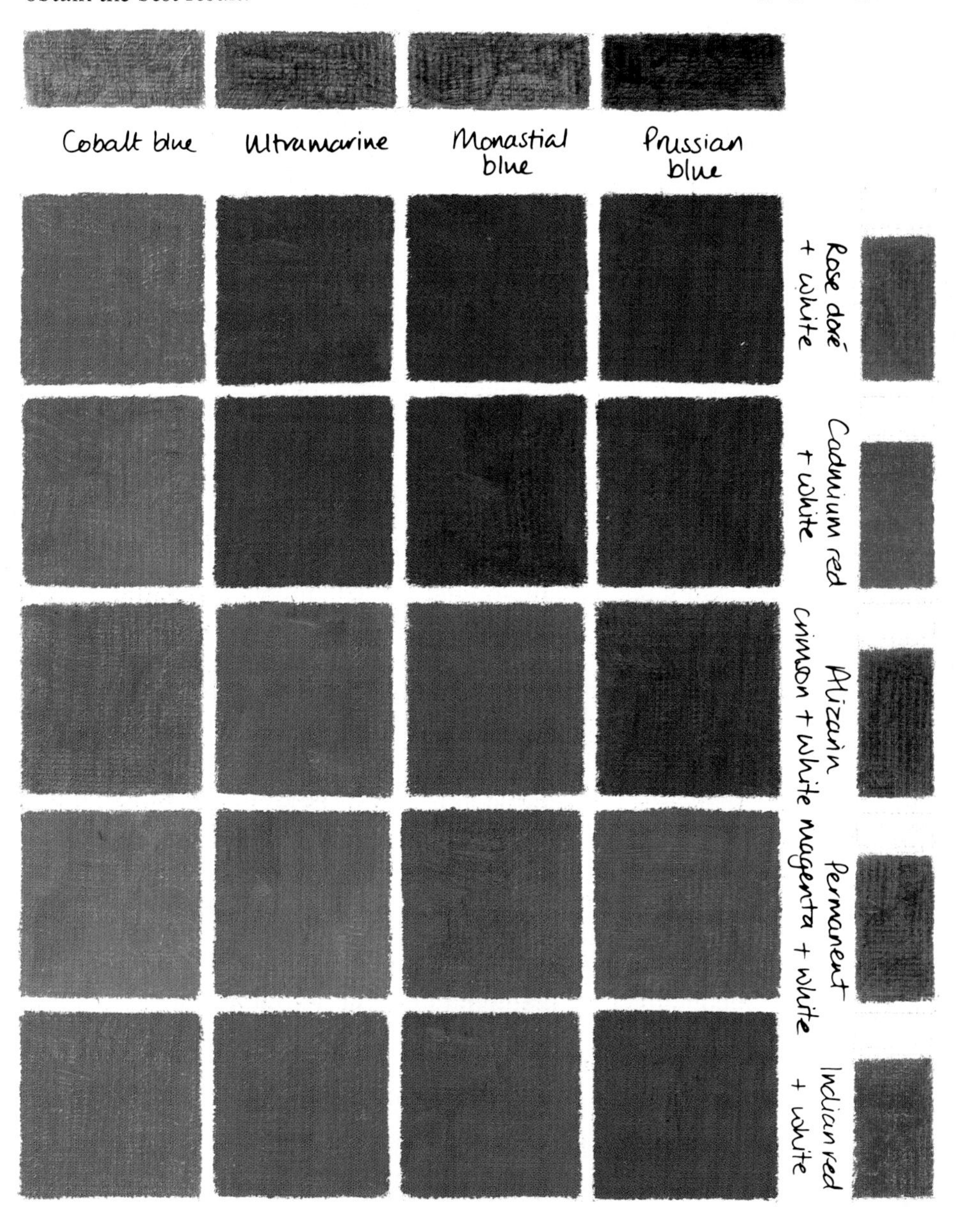
Cobalt blue
Ultramarine
Monastial blue
Prussian blue
Rose doré + white
Cadmium red + white
Alizarin crimson + white
Permanent magenta + white
Indian red + white

USING ORANGES AND PURPLES

Stewart Geddes – *Kensal Road, Bristol*

34 × 32 ins

LIKE ALL THE PAINTINGS in the book, this was done direct from the subject. It is on canvas, which was first given a warm pinkish ground made from Indian red, yellow ochre and white. An underdrawing was made in charcoal, and before painting this was fixed to prevent the charcoal muddying the paint. The painting was then completed rapidly to catch the fleeting effects of light and colour.

► *For the sky, permanent magenta, cobalt blue and white have been painted loosely over the pink ground, parts of which have been allowed to show through. The distant buildings are a mix of cadmium red, chrome yellow, Indian red, raw umber and white.*

▼ *A mixture of Indian red and raw umber has been used for the deep shadow at the end of the terrace.*

▲ *The side of the house is a mixture of Indian red and cobalt blue with a little white; the fronts of the terrace are chrome yellow and white; the rooftops are cadmium red, raw umber and white.*

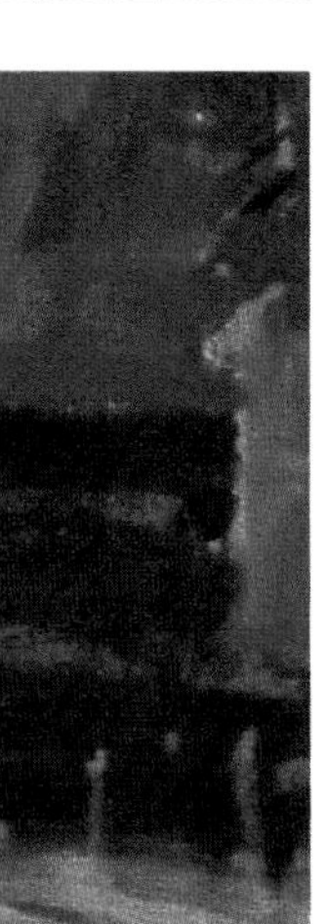

◄ *For this very dark shadow, cobalt blue has been added to the Indian red and raw umber mixture. In front, chrome yellow with a little white highlights the pavement.*

◄ *For this shadow area, mixtures of cobalt blue, permanent magenta, raw umber, Indian red and white have been used. A dashing stroke of ultramarine mixed with white contrasts with the more sombre purples and reds.*

Viridian

Lemon yellow
Cadmium yellow
Cadmium red
Alizarin crimson
Ultramarine
Cobalt blue
Viridian
Sap green
Yellow ochre
Burnt sienna
Raw umber
Ivory black

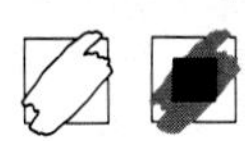

Sap green

Lemon yellow | Cadmium yellow | Cadmium red | Alizarin crimson

Ultramarine | Cobalt blue | Viridian | Sap green

Yellow ochre | Burnt sienna | Raw umber | Ivory black

Cobalt green

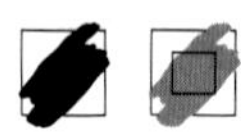

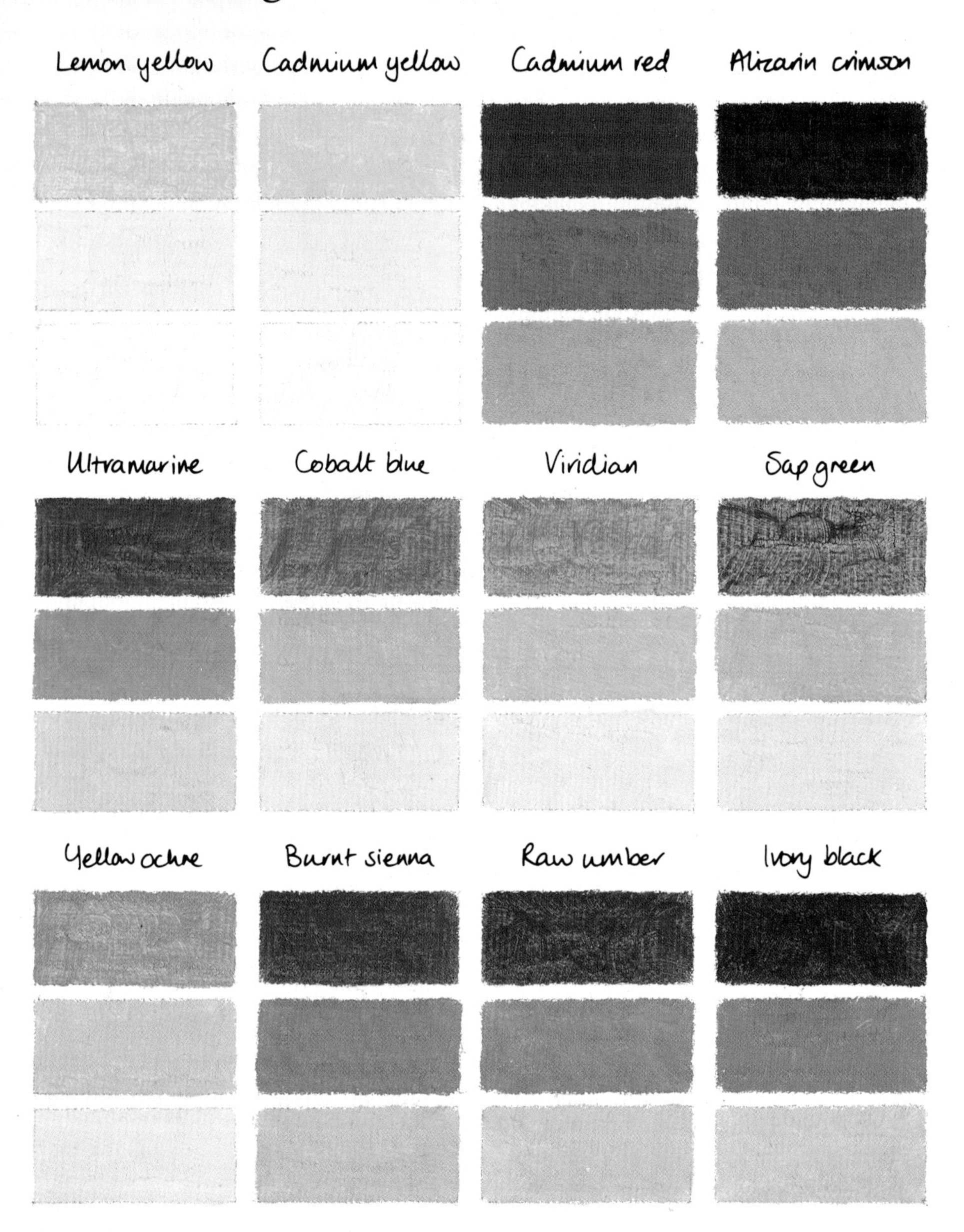
Lemon yellow
Cadmium yellow
Cadmium red
Alizarin crimson
Ultramarine
Cobalt blue
Viridian
Sap green
Yellow ochre
Burnt sienna
Raw umber
Ivory black

Oxide of chromium green

Lemon yellow

Cadmium yellow

Cadmium red

Alizarin crimson

Ultramarine

Cobalt blue

Viridian

Sap green

Yellow ochre

Burnt sienna

Raw umber

Ivory black

Mixing greens

As mentioned on pages 6-7, mixed secondaries are not generally as

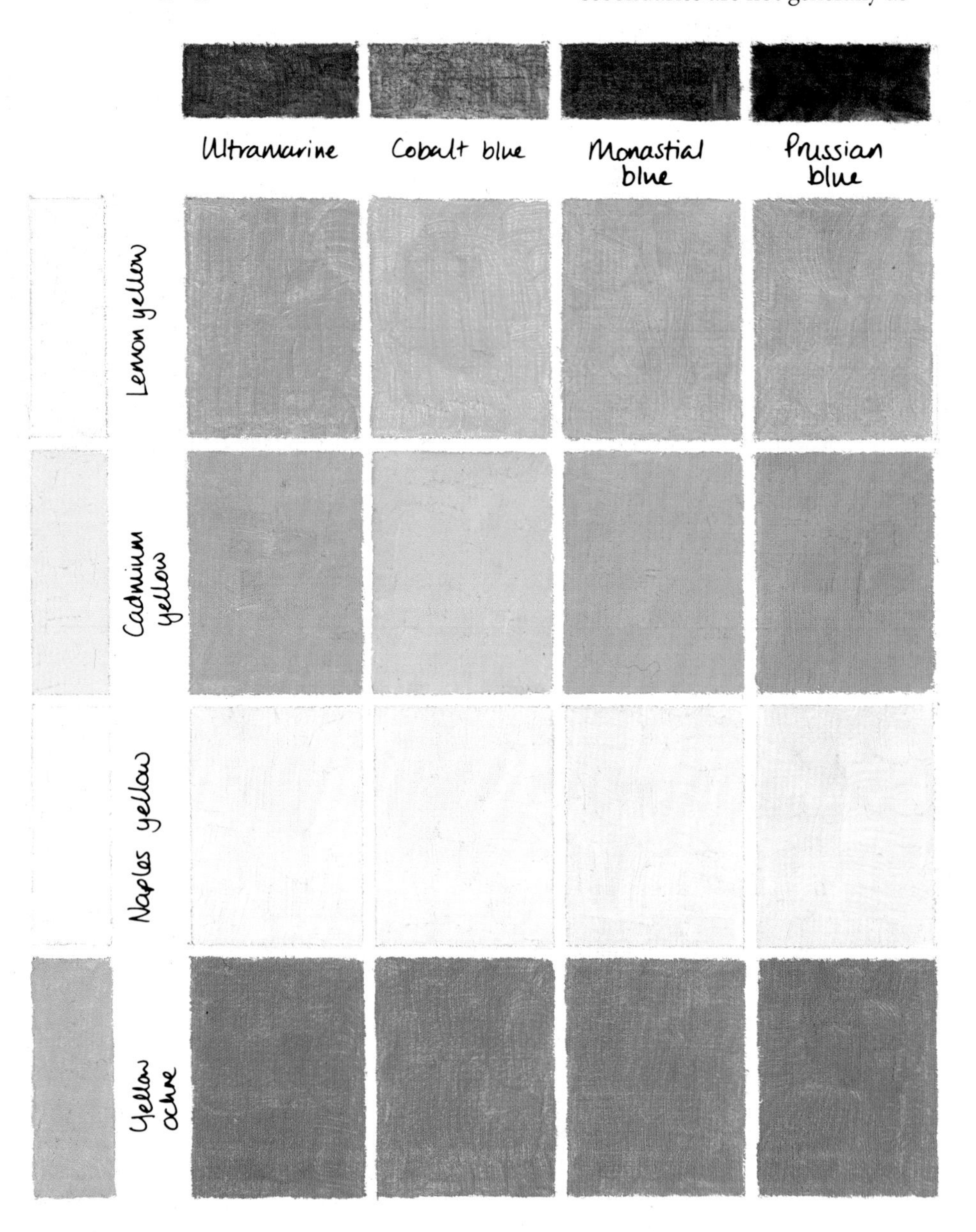
Ultramarine
Cobalt blue
Monastial blue
Prussian blue
Lemon yellow
Cadmium yellow
Naples yellow
Yellow ochre

bright as those purchased in a tube. In the case of greens, however, certain mixes of blue and yellow produce vivid greens.

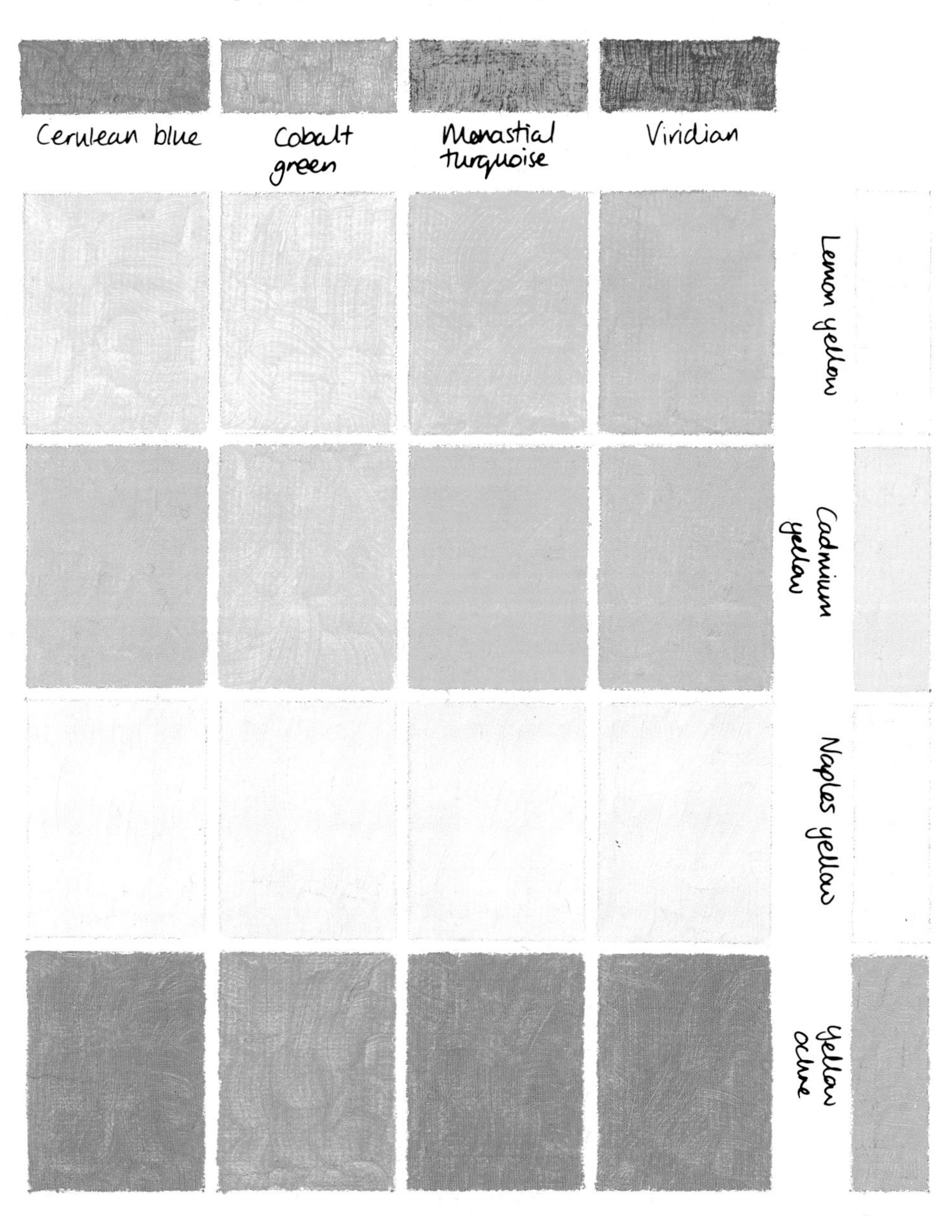

Cerulean blue
Cobalt green
Monastial turquoise
Viridian
Lemon yellow
Cadmium yellow
Naples yellow
Yellow ochre

Using Greens

Robert Maxwell-Wood – *Sunflowers*

18 × 14 ins

BOTH GREENS AND YELLOWS are slightly muted, but the painting is lively and full of movement, due in part to the contrast of small, linear marks of dark paint and broad slabs of colour. The painting was done with bristle brushes on canvas.

► *The greens used for the back of this sunflower were mixed from cadmium yellow, lemon yellow, ultramarine, cadmium green, cadmium red and cobalt blue. The stalk bears traces of cadmium yellow and a pale bluish green mixed from lemon yellow, cerulean blue and white.*

▼ *The greenish browns in the centre of the flower are made from cadmium yellow, cadmium orange, ultramarine, viridian and cadmium red.*

▲ *The pale green here consists of white, cerulean and cadmium yellow, while the darker green has been made by adding cadmium red, oxide of chromium green and a touch of viridian.*

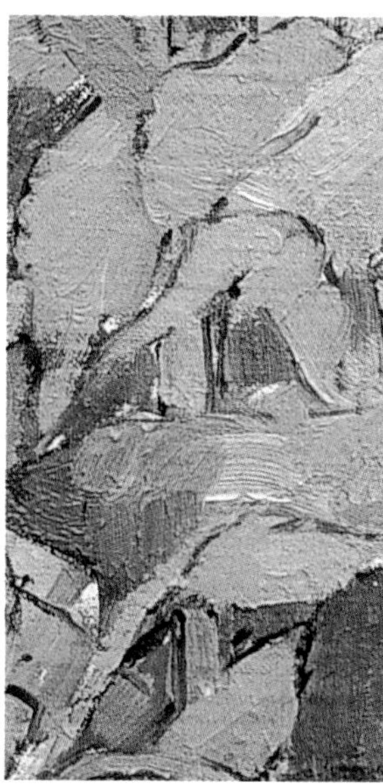

◄ *These bright yellowish greens have been mixed from lemon yellow and cerulean blue.*

Lemon yellow

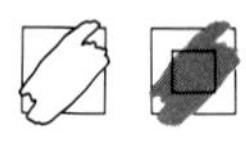

Lemon yellow	Cadmium yellow	Cadmium red	Alizarin crimson
Ultramarine	Cobalt blue	Viridian	Sap green
Yellow ochre	Burnt sienna	Raw umber	Ivory black

Cadmium yellow

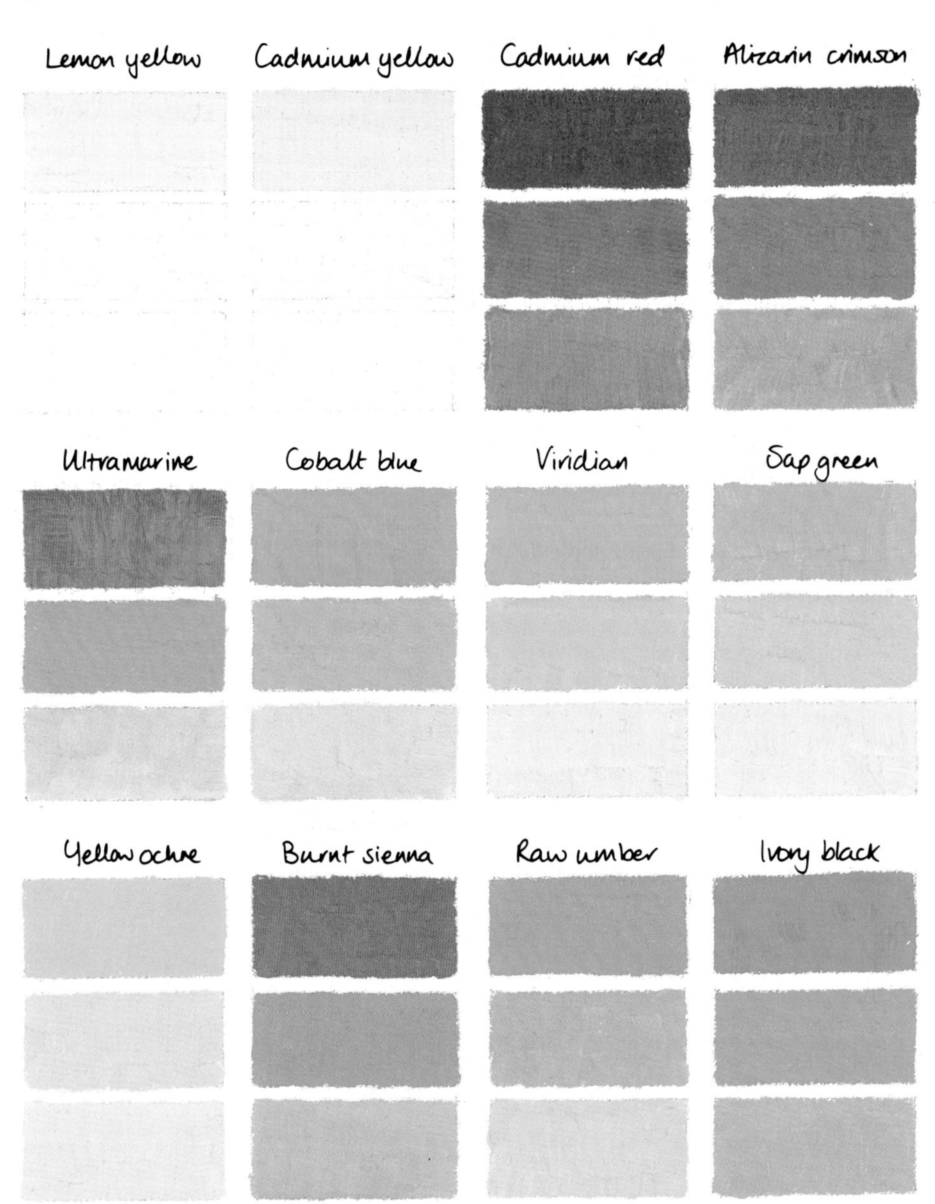
Lemon yellow
Cadmium yellow
Cadmium red
Alizarin crimson
Ultramarine
Cobalt blue
Viridian
Sap green
Yellow ochre
Burnt sienna
Raw umber
Ivory black

Naples yellow

Lemon yellow

Cadmium yellow

Cadmium red

Alizarin crimson

Ultramarine

Cobalt blue

Viridian

Sap green

Yellow ochre

Burnt sienna

Raw umber

Ivory black

Cadmium orange

Lemon yellow
Cadmium yellow
Cadmium red
Alizarin crimson
Ultramarine
Cobalt blue
Viridian
Sap green
Yellow ochre
Burnt sienna
Raw umber
Ivory black

Yellow ochre

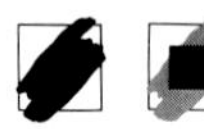

Lemon yellow
Cadmium yellow
Cadmium red
Alizarin crimson
Ultramarine
Cobalt blue
Viridian
Sap green
Yellow ochre
Burnt sienna
Raw umber
Ivory black

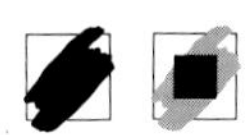

Raw sienna

Lemon yellow
Cadmium yellow
Cadmium red
Alizarin crimson
Ultramarine
Cobalt blue
Viridian
Sap green
Yellow ochre
Burnt sienna
Raw umber
Ivory black

Mixing browns

Browns are tertiary colours (see pages 6-7). The charts below

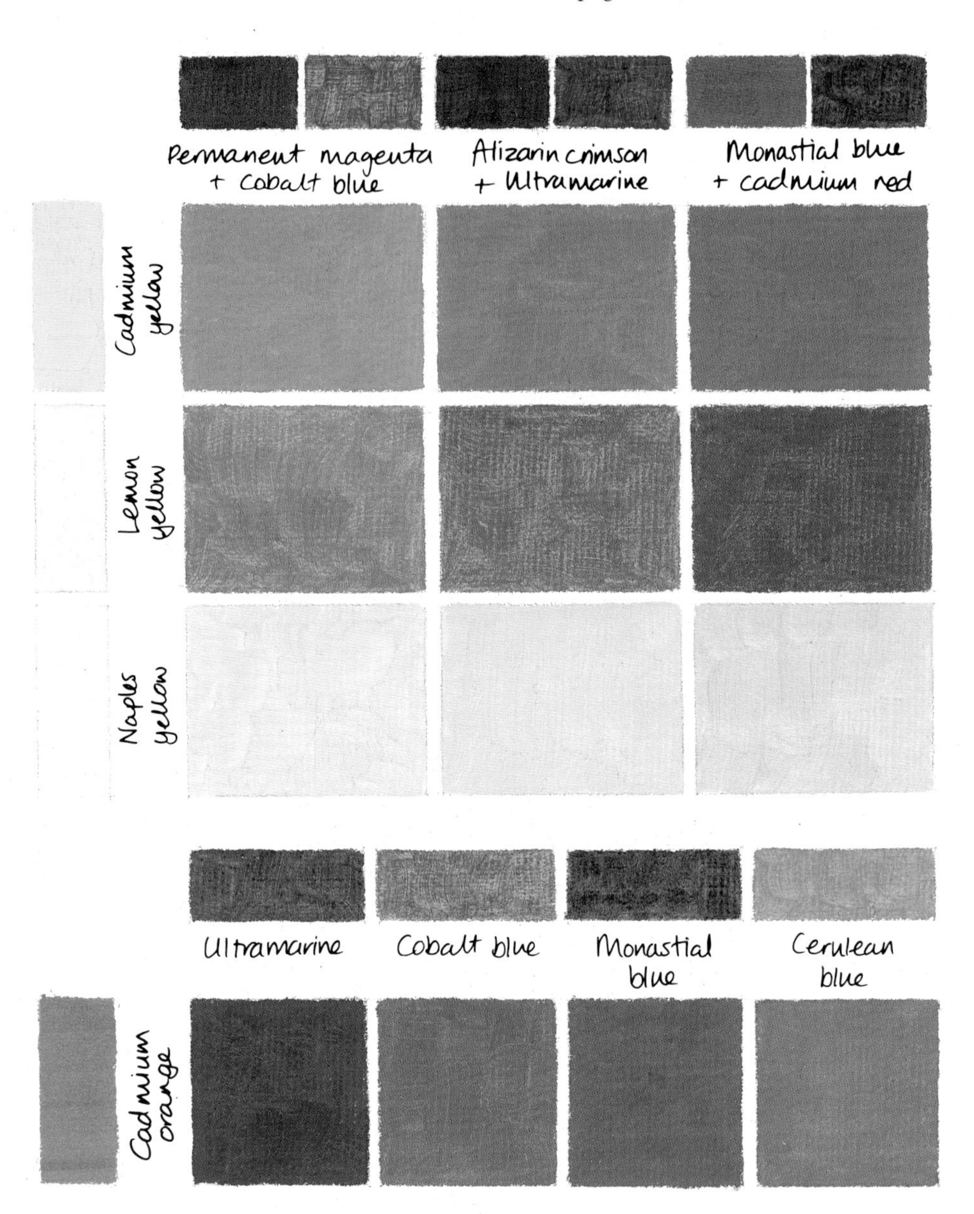
Permanent magenta + Cobalt blue
Alizarin crimson + Ultramarine
Monastial blue + cadmium red
Cadmium yellow
Lemon yellow
Naples yellow
Ultramarine
Cobalt blue
Monastial blue
Cerulean blue
Cadmium orange

show ways of making browns from the three pairs of complementary colours.

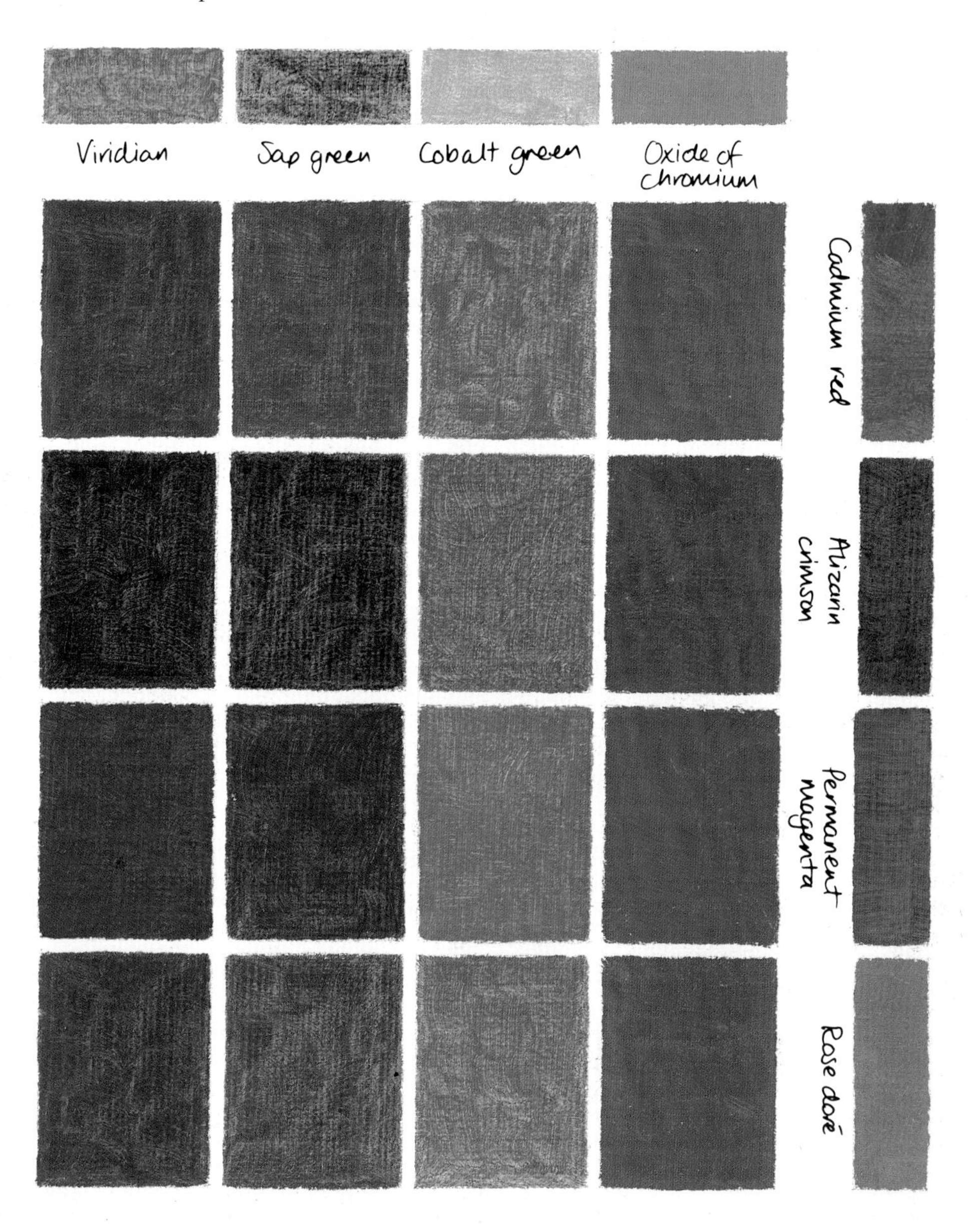
Viridian
Sap green
Cobalt green
Oxide of chromium
Cadmium red
Alizarin crimson
Permanent magenta
Rose doré

USING BROWNS

Gerald Cains – *Autumn Ploughing*

30×28 ins

BOTH BRISTLE BRUSHES and painting knives have been used here, and the paint has been applied thickly. To help it dry more quickly, a synthetic painting medium called Liquin was added. The composition was first blocked in with a painting knife and then completed rapidly during deteriorating weather conditions.

▼ *For the ploughed strip at the top, mixes of ultramarine, Indian red, yellow ochre and white have been used, and the nearer field has been painted with viridian, Naples yellow and white, yellow ochre and white, and small amounts of Vandyke brown.*

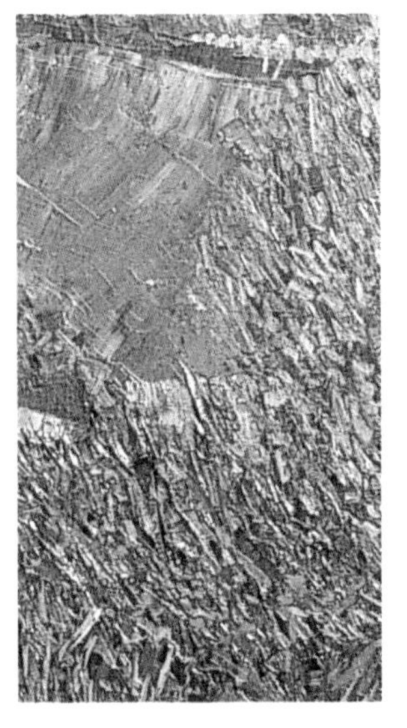

◀ *Open strokes of colour have been used for this pale tree, painted with varying proportions of Naples yellow, yellow ochre, viridian, lamp black, cadmium red and white.*

▼ *The texture of the foreground field has been suggested with slabs and slashes of the painting knife, with the colours only partially mixed. The colours are Indian red, yellow ochre, cobalt blue, Vandyke brown, burnt umber and alizarin crimson.*

◀ *Distant furrows have been painted with mixtures of Vandyke brown, lamp black, ultramarine, Indian red, alizarin crimson and white. Some artists dislike using black, but it can be very useful in mixtures.*

Cadmium red

Lemon yellow	Cadmium yellow	Cadmium red	Alizarin crimson

Ultramarine	Cobalt blue	Viridian	Sap green

Yellow ochre	Burnt sienna	Raw umber	Ivory black

Alizarin crimson

Lemon yellow
Cadmium yellow
Cadmium red
Alizarin crimson
Ultramarine
Cobalt blue
Viridian
Sap green
Yellow ochre
Burnt sienna
Raw umber
Ivory black

Indian red

Lemon yellow | Cadmium yellow | Cadmium red | Alizarin crimson

Ultramarine | Cobalt blue | Viridian | Sap green

Yellow ochre | Burnt sienna | Raw umber | Ivory black

Mars violet

Lemon yellow

Cadmium yellow

Cadmium red

Alizarin crimson

Ultramarine

Cobalt blue

Viridian

Sap green

Yellow ochre

Burnt sienna

Raw umber

Ivory black

Venetian red

Lemon yellow	Cadmium yellow	Cadmium red	Alizarin crimson
Ultramarine	**Cobalt blue**	**Viridian**	**Sap green**
Yellow ochre	**Burnt sienna**	**Raw umber**	**Ivory black**

Rose doré

Lemon yellow
Cadmium yellow
Cadmium red
Alizarin crimson
Ultramarine
Cobalt blue
Viridian
Sap green
Yellow ochre
Burnt sienna
Raw umber
Ivory black

Mixing skin tones

The number of different words we use for describing the colour of skin – cream, peaches, gold, coffee, ebony and so on – points up the fact that skin tones vary widely. In addition, the colours are affected by lighting conditions and surrounding colours,

Very dark *Complexion*

Alizarin crimson with raw umber and Prussian blue

Shadows

Alizarin crimson + Prussian blue

Alizarin crimson + viridian

Payne's grey

Highlights

Naples yellow

Cadmium red + white

Cobalt blue + white

Mid-brown *Complexion*

Burnt umber, yellow ochre, cadmium orange + white

Shadows

Raw umber

Ultramarine

Raw umber + cadmium red

Highlights

Cadmium yellow + white

Lemon yellow + white

Cadmium red + white

particularly of clothing. It is at least as important to pitch the tones (the lights and darks) correctly as to find the "right" colours, and artists often take liberties with colours to achieve effects that, while not strictly realistic, may enhance the appearance of living flesh. But although it is not possible to suggest a suitable palette for all skin, some suggestions can be made. Here we show four suggested basic colours, to which further colours can be added for shadows and highlights.

Olive *Complexion*

Yellow ochre + white

Shadows

Cadmium red + raw umber

Raw sienna + cobalt blue

Permanent mauve

Highlights

Lemon yellow + white

Cadmium yellow + white

Cerulean blue + White

Pale *Complexion*

Yellow ochre, rose doré + white

Shadows

Cadmium red + cobalt blue

Alizarin crimson + raw umber

Cerulean blue + cadmium red

Highlights

White

Naples yellow

White + Lemon yellow

USING SKIN TONES

Rosalind Cuthbert – *Ray and Moya Trapnell*

42 × 30 ins

THIS HIGHLY DETAILED PAINTING on canvas took several sittings. The composition was first drawn with a fine brush and well-diluted paint, and then built up gradually. To achieve the subtle variations of colour in the flesh tints, clothing and background, a fairly extensive palette has been used.

◀ *The paler complexion of the woman was built up with mixes of rose doré, yellow ochre and white, and the shadowed sides are worked with strokes of raw umber, rose doré and cadmium red mixtures, with very small touches of magenta and cobalt blue.*

▶ *The man's suntanned face has been painted with mixes of white, yellow ochre, Indian red, cadmium red, alizarin crimson and raw umber. Highlights contain more yellow ochre and white, and shadowed areas more raw umber plus an addition of burnt umber.*

B.TRAPNELL & SONS
Coal Merchants
Over 60 Years
ROAD W-S-M

Permanent magenta

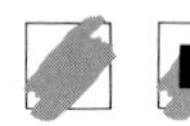

Lemon yellow
Cadmium yellow
Cadmium red
Alizarin crimson
Ultramarine
Cobalt blue
Viridian
Sap green
Yellow ochre
Burnt sienna
Raw umber
Ivory black

Permanent mauve

Lemon yellow
Cadmium yellow
Cadmium red
Alizarin crimson
Ultramarine
Cobalt blue
Viridian
Sap green
Yellow ochre
Burnt sienna
Raw umber
Ivory black

Burnt umber

Lemon yellow

Cadmium yellow

Cadmium red

Alizarin crimson

Ultramarine

Cobalt blue

Viridian

Sap green

Yellow ochre

Burnt sienna

Raw umber

Ivory black

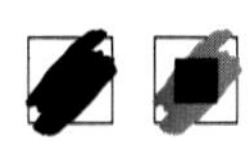

Raw umber

Lemon yellow
Cadmium yellow
Cadmium red
Alizarin crimson
Ultramarine
Cobalt blue
Viridian
Sap green
Yellow ochre
Burnt sienna
Raw umber
Ivory black

Burnt sienna

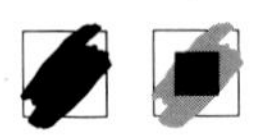

Lemon yellow
Cadmium yellow
Cadmium red
Alizarin crimson
Ultramarine
Cobalt blue
Viridian
Sap green
Yellow ochre
Burnt sienna
Raw umber
Ivory black

Vandyke brown

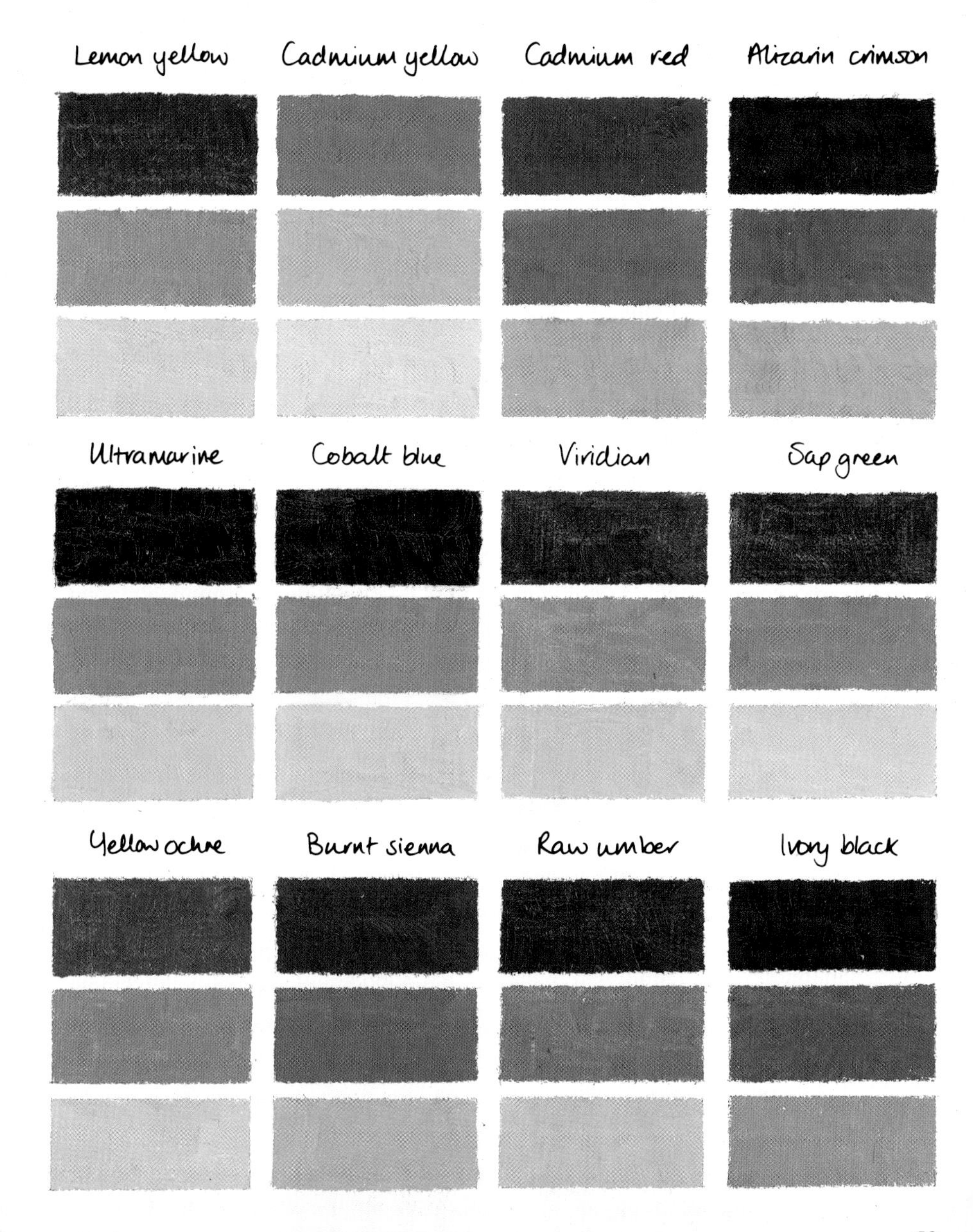
Lemon yellow
Cadmium yellow
Cadmium red
Alizarin crimson
Ultramarine
Cobalt blue
Viridian
Sap green
Yellow ochre
Burnt sienna
Raw umber
Ivory black

Mixing greys

Greys, like browns, are tertiary colours (see pages 6-7), and can

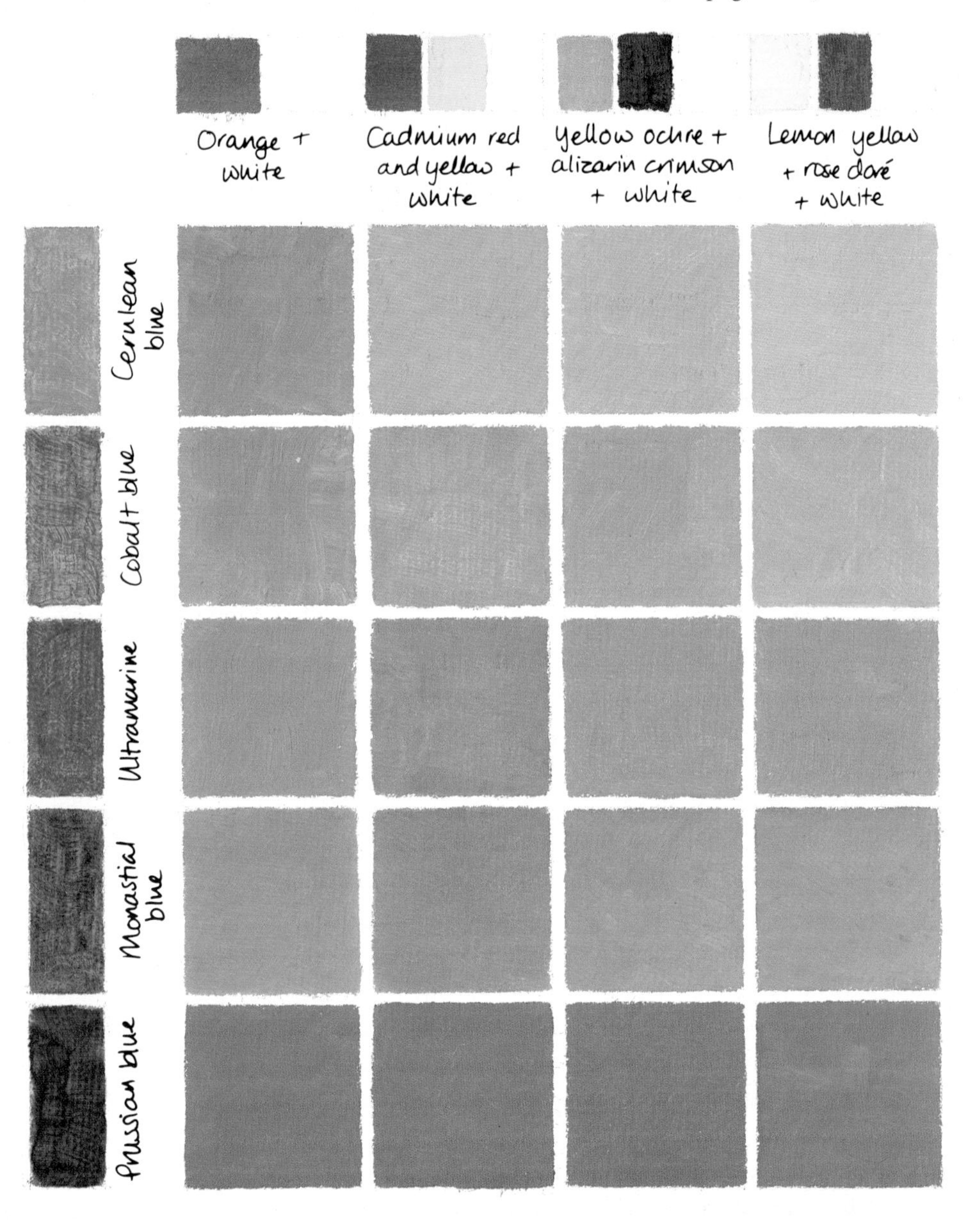

Orange + white
Cadmium red and yellow + white
Yellow ochre + alizarin crimson + white
Lemon yellow + rose doré + white
Cerulean blue
Cobalt blue
Ultramarine
Monastial blue
Prussian blue

usually be mixed by emphasizing the blue content and adding white in varying degrees.

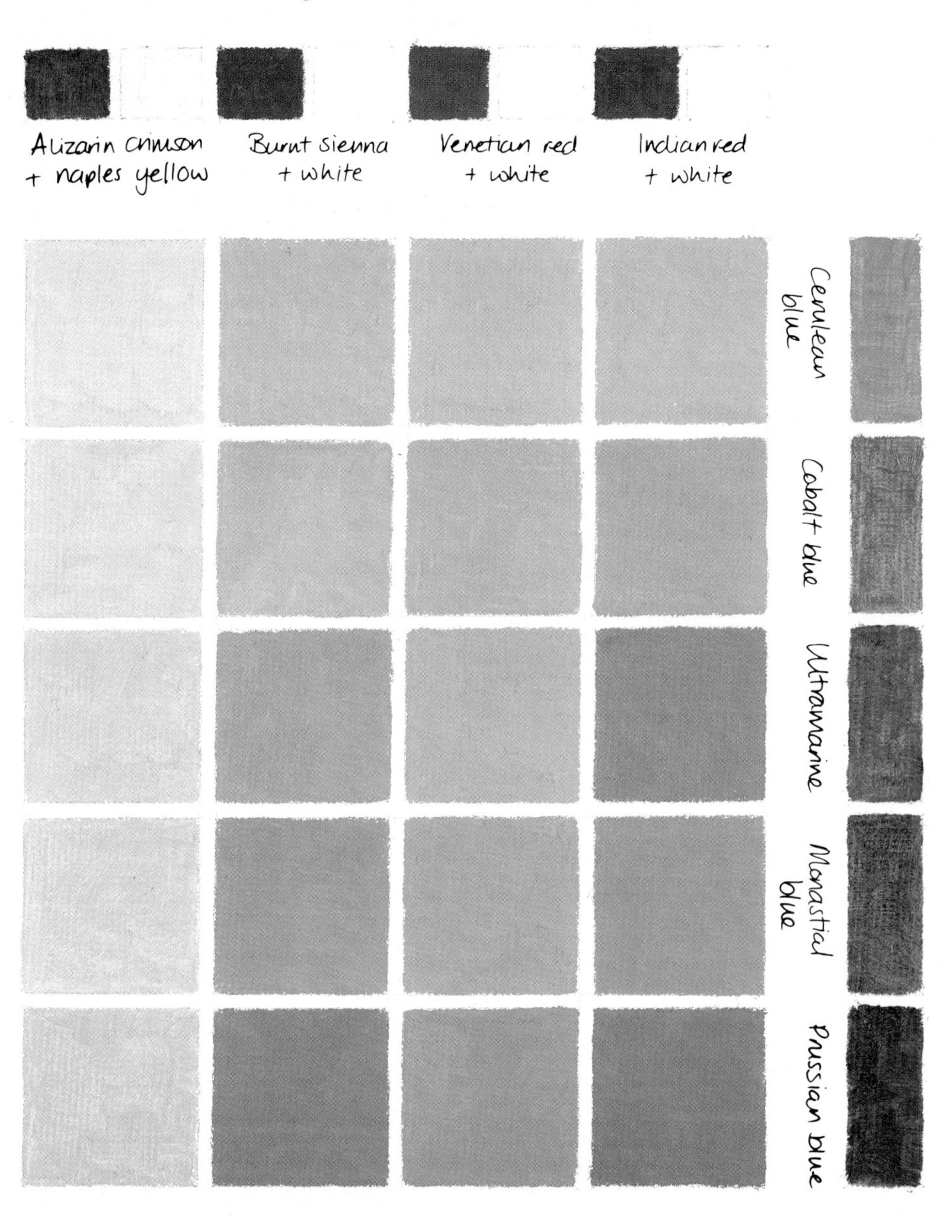

Alizarin crimson + naples yellow
Burnt sienna + white
Venetian red + white
Indian red + white
Cerulean blue
Cobalt blue
Ultramarine
Monastial blue
Prussian blue

Using Greys

Eve Quarmby – *Primroses*

18 × 14 ins

THIS PICTURE has been painted on canvas board using bristle brushes. Although the colour scheme is cool, a wide range of yellows and browns has been used – Naples yellow, lemon yellow, cadmium yellow, yellow ochre, raw sienna, raw umber and burnt sienna – and only one blue, ultramarine. The colour has been applied quite thinly, using pure turpentine with a little linseed oil. The colours are restrained and delicate, in keeping with the subject.

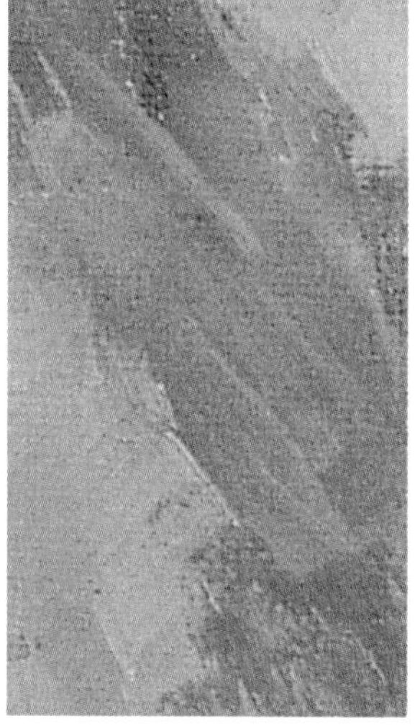

► *The yellow-brown ambiguous shape balances the downward pull of the strong form just below. This corner, using greys mixed from ultramarine, raw umber, yellow ochre and white, is important in creating a gentle, intimate space around the flowers.*

▼ *The pale greys suggesting shade on the primroses have been mixed with ultramarine, burnt sienna, Naples yellow and white.*

▲ *The darker cool greys have been mixed with raw umber, ultramarine and white, while the greyish pink uses raw umber, cadmium red, ultramarine and white.*

◄ *Yellow ochre, raw umber and white form the basis of the neutral yellowish drape. For the shadow, a small amount of ultramarine mixed with raw umber and white has been blended into the yellowish colour.*

Payne's grey

Lemon yellow

Cadmium yellow

Cadmium red

Alizarin crimson

Ultramarine

Cobalt blue

Viridian

Sap green

Yellow ochre

Burnt sienna

Raw umber

Ivory black

Ivory black

Lemon yellow
Cadmium yellow
Cadmium red
Alizarin crimson
Ultramarine
Cobalt blue
Viridian
Sap green
Yellow ochre
Burnt sienna
Raw umber
Ivory black

Overpainting with transparent colours

In the early days of oil painting, colours were built up with transparent paint, used in a layering technique. Overpainting with transparent colours, called glazing, can be useful for

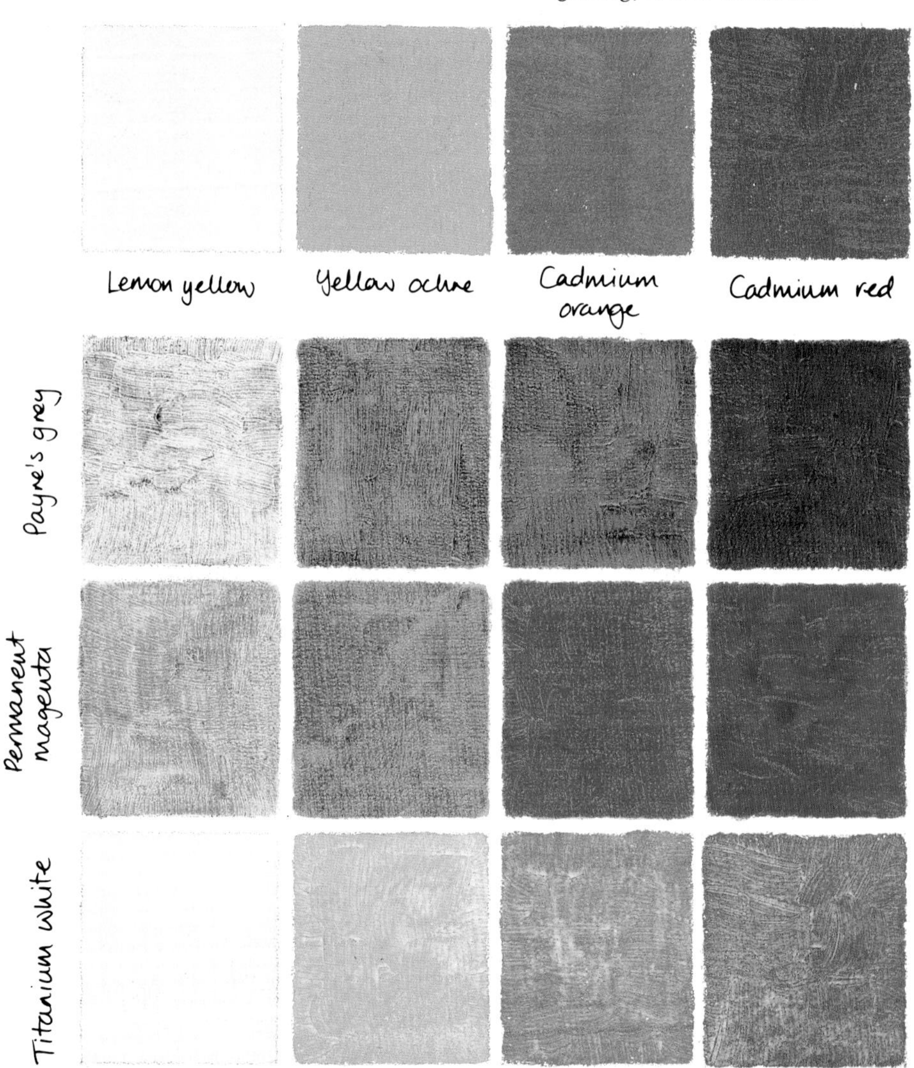

Lemon yellow
Yellow ochre
Cadmium orange
Cadmium red
Payne's grey
Permanent magenta
Titanium white

modifying and adjusting colours already put down, and it also adds to the range of possible effects. You can glaze over thick or thin paint as long as the previous layer is completely dry. To make the colours transparent, they should be mixed with a special medium called glazing medium, available from most good art shops, not with linseed oil.

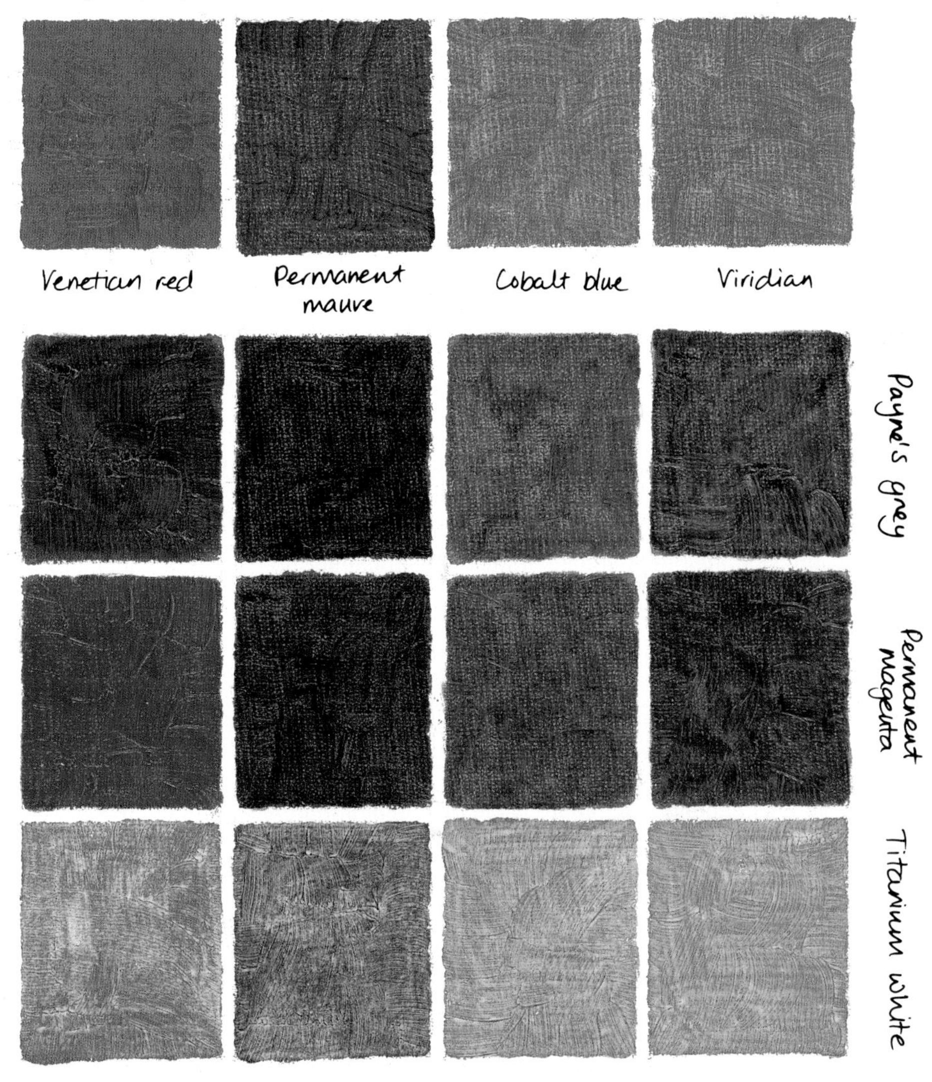

Venetian red
Permanent mauve
Cobalt blue
Viridian
Payne's grey
Permanent Magenta
Titanium white

Optical mixing

The French painter Georges Seurat and others used to put small dabs or strokes of contrasting colours next to each other on the canvas, so that from a distance they would "mix" in the eye of the viewer. This, called

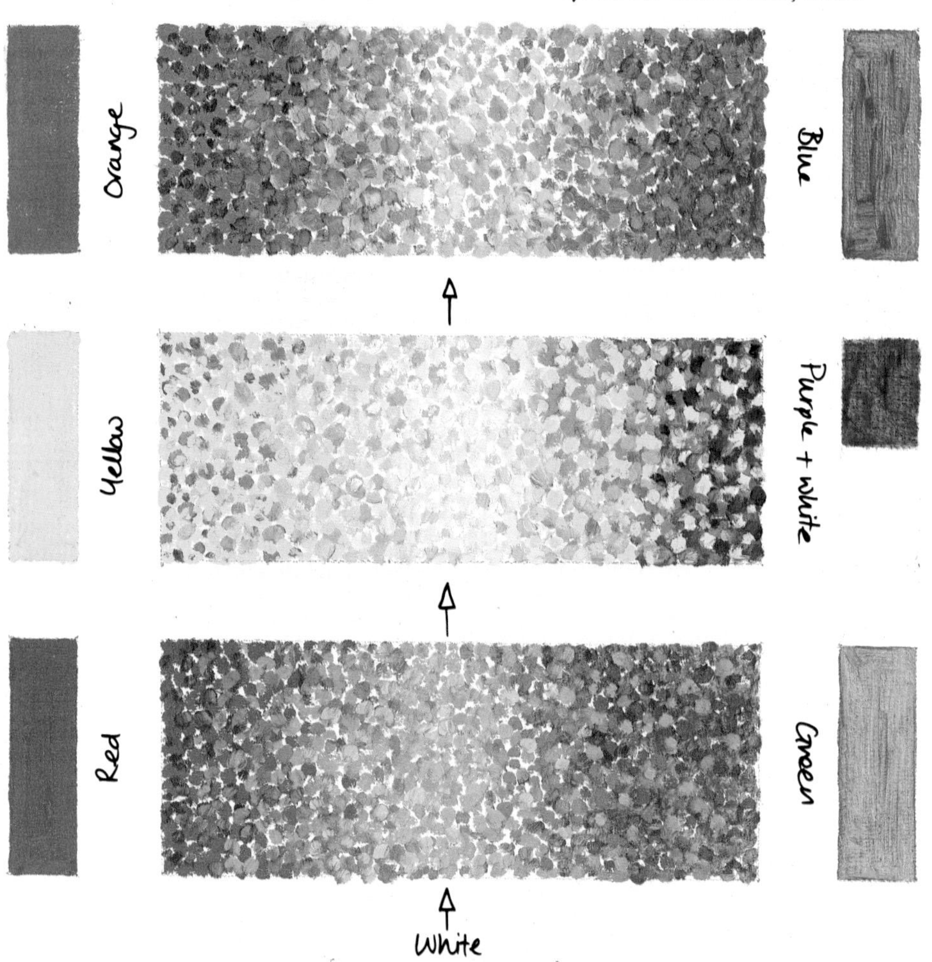

Orange
Blue
Yellow
Purple + white
Red
Green
White

Pointillism, creates a lively impression, and modified versions of the technique are still used today. For the best results, the colours must be close in tone (i.e. of a similar lightness or darkness). Here are some examples – you may need to hold the book away from you so that the "optical mixing" can take place.

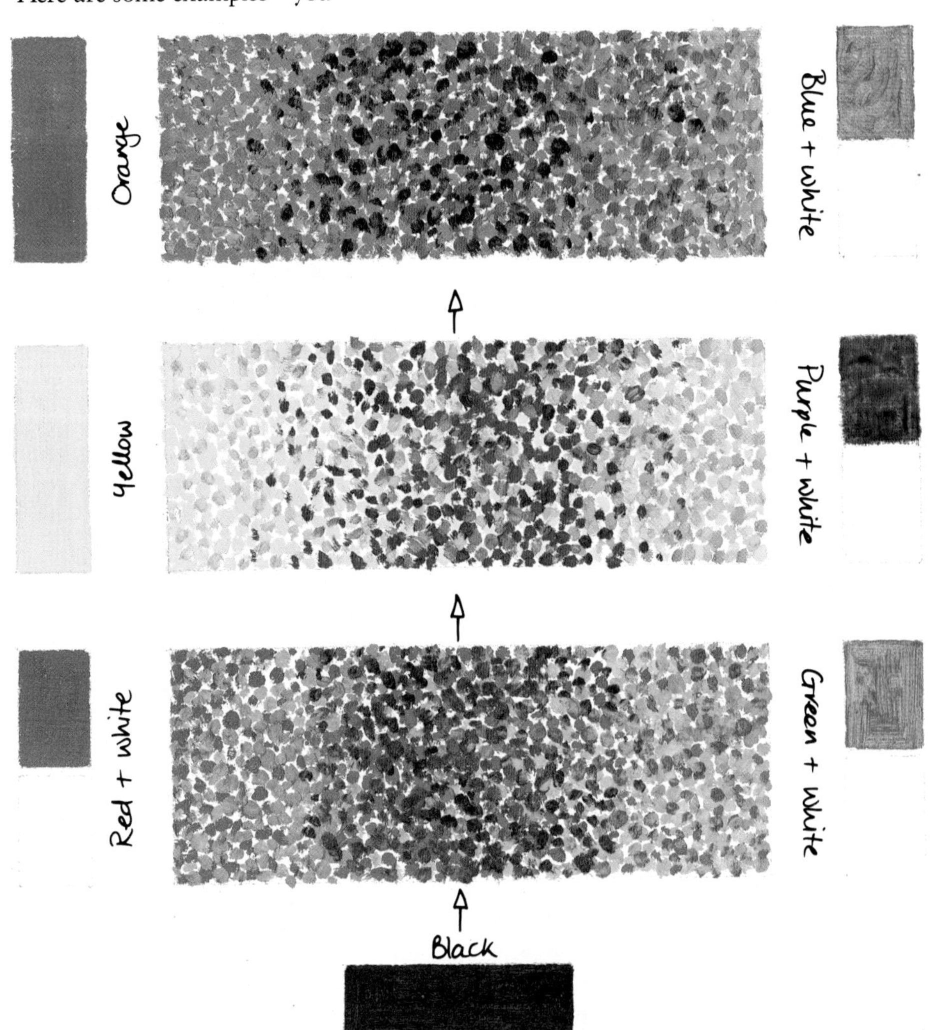
Orange
Blue + white
Yellow
Purple + white
Red + white
Green + white
Black

CREDITS

CONTRIBUTING ARTISTS
18 Stewart Geddes; **26** Robert Maxwell-Wood;
36 Gerald Cains; **44** Rosalind Cuthbert;
56 Eve Quarmby

Senior Editor
Hazel Harrison

Senior Art Editor
Penny Cobb

Design Assistant
Clare Baggaley

Typeset by West End Studios, Eastbourne

The publishers would like to thank
Daler-Rowney Limited for their generosity
in supplying artist's materials

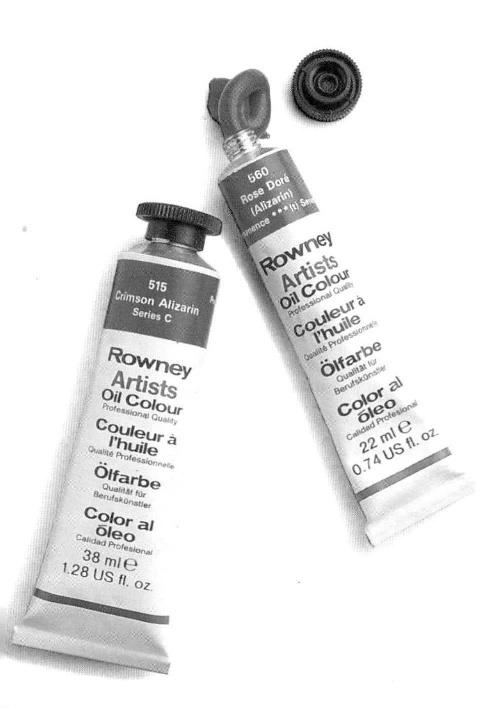
515
Crimson Alizarin
Series C
Rowney
Artists
Oil Colour
Professional Quality
Couleur à
l'huile
Qualité Professionnelle
Ölfarbe
Qualität für
Berufskünstler
Color al
óleo
Calidad Profesional
38 ml ℮
1.28 US fl. oz.
560
Rose Doré
(Alizarin)
Rowney
Artists
Oil Colour
Professional Quality
Couleur à
l'huile
Ölfarbe
Qualität für
Berufskünstler
Color al
óleo
Calidad Profesional
22 ml ℮
0.74 US fl. oz.